fortunate
by
kim rashidi

© 2021 kim rashidi.
bykimrashidi@gmail.com

cover artist:
giavannasart@gmail.com

ISBN 978-1-72569-270-1

dear reader,

thank you for being here and stepping into my spiritual book of poetry. though you are a reader of these poems, you will also act as a reader of tarot. the poems here are always mystical and at times cryptic. you will have to *read* into the words and in between the lines to create meaning for yourself (and to connect these poems to your own life). i recommend flipping to a random page whenever you feel that you need some guidance, or are called to receive a message. different parts of different poems will stick out to you at different times. my intention with this book is to offer my own intuition and allow you to connect with yours. use the blank pages beside each poem as a place to express yourself: draw, scribble, write, and scratch to your heart's desire. you may also use those pages to reflect or claim a certain feeling or vibe that you *read* in a poem. do whatever brings you peace. i'll leave you with that.

with love,
kimmy

fortunate

EIGHT OF WANDS

with the way comes the worry,
but don't forget the journey.

just as water runs
/even in still rivers/
the freedom to move
is what you're built for.

follow through
and let your intuition
show you where to
make do.

PAGE OF PENTACLES

your outer is your inner,
what you see is real,
and what you feel, realer.

if material abundance
is what you seek,
then align your worlds
and speak of the life you
wish to lead.

fortunate

THREE OF CUPS

just as you have talents to offer,
others have some to share,

gather and birth your ideas
to their heirs;

a trio is ever-more satisfying
than can be a solo-affair.

fortunate

ACE OF SWORDS

new!
perspectives and ideas are in town;

do you see things shine in varying ways?

with an open mind,
welcome the answers,

let them shine through
and nurture one little seed
into the bean-stalk of
your dreams.

fortunate

PAGE OF CUPS

do you have what it takes to look within?
even if you don't know where to begin?

explore the depths of this new spark,
offer some patience and it
will blossom with luck.

signs swarm all around,
but it's up to you to
claim them as found.

ACE OF CUPS

you radiate who you are with
such confidence
that the tips of your
fingers leave the trail of
personality
wherever they go.

give what you can,
and take even less—

be it love or kindness,
make this connection last;

be it neural or human,
take it in the palm of your hands,

and rest at ease knowing that you
are on the right path.

kim rashidi

fortunate

KNIGHT OF PENTACLES

time,
you have so much of it left,
be it an hour or decades ahead.

look around you
and make meaning for yourself,

the work you put in
is the life that comes out.

the course you've set out on is right
for right now:
your vehicle, your itinerary.

follow your plan
to come out unscathed.

fortunate

dip your toes into the water.
getting a taste of what's
to come will fuel your passion
to tread on.

you see two paths, oh so clearly,
but the third one,
 the one in between,
reveals itself once you rise
to the challenge of finding balance.

to create what you desire,
mix your options until you find your fire.

fortunate

surrounded by gold,
your value shines through.
you learned the lessons,
mastered the arts, and
found new ways to see this life.

"what's next?" you ask.

hold on to the creativity you struck,
logic and emotion flow
perfectly equal in your cup.

maintain your mastery
and contain harmony,
life will proceed as it shall be.

kim rashidi

fortunate

DEATH

the sun sets every day
only to be reborn the next.

(1) one new message.

a carrier brings in news, a change, a
rebirth.

in his path remains a transition:
what was has served its purpose,
and what is will serve its own, too.

just as the sun whispers a daily
colourful *adieu,* so must you.

celebrate what you had!
prepare for what's ahead.

kim rashidi

fortunate

dealing with a loss, or a story about it,
know that you are never alone.

let go of the fear
of not having enough;

strife is ever-present
and bleak winters never cease;

and yet,
spring always comes,
rain brings shine,
and flowers breathe life.

kim rashidi

fortunate

you placed your roots,
and look how they flourished!

a flower sits in each area of life
just to show you the light.
share some of your petals,
and you'll never have to settle.

* * *

people from the past
snake into the present,

so, ask yourself
if you mesh;
if not, let go—
both of mind
and flesh.

kim rashidi

12

fortunate

though you juggle more
things than one
 all at once,
you do so because you can.

but while you fulfill your duties,
life outside of your
responsibilities
goes on.

manage your time
and leave some out,   (just for you)
fall into nothingness
and out of doubt.

kim rashidi

13

KNIGHT OF WANDS

a fire illuminates your task
and you jump into action,

now, keep going and start
a new tradition.

you have the how and the why in
your favour,

though a scheme should
precede your endeavour:

venture off and take the route
that seems fitting,

and if this sounds too hard, remember
that *value* requires committing.

fortunate

KNIGHT OF CUPS

water creatures crawl
at the surface
of your mind,
your creativity is at an all-time high.

as a charm for all things beautiful:

your channeled inspiration
sways still rivers, and
your enchanting intuition
acts as the giver.

THREE OF SWORDS

a cloudy day is just that:
a day—a fleeting experience.

know that others' words are mere
reflections of who they are.
your worth doesn't disintegrate
with a few swords to the heart,

negative self-talk deceives you
from time to time, so stand up to
yourself, and just *be* who you are.

a new day always starts.

THE DEVIL

two choices/two people
sit opposite one another,
and then
    a third figure, a reflected one:

big with	and
secrets	experiences
you've *	you've
held	pressed
onto,	into.

but, you already know this.
awareness gives you a task:
break the reflection into pieces,
and bring light
to shadows by addressing them;

illuminating
the unknown reveals a new realm.

kim rashidi

fortunate

KING OF WANDS

gold embroidered, your options
are carefully considered.

a chapter of realistic thought,
you lead the way, and others
follow at no cost.

your role is dignified,
and you do what it takes
to be recognized.

whatever you're stepping into,
now is your time to shine.

remember to live with purpose,
even if that purpose is to align

with who you *are*.

fortunate

QUEEN OF SWORDS

you've got your head up high,
high in the clouds,
all perched up.

now all you need to do is perk up.

you sit alone, fair but calm.
they see the light in you,
the one you fight to keep on.

all that remains is
to celebrate your wins
and to show up for yourself
day after day.

kim rashidi

fortunate

SEVEN OF PENTACLES

sometimes accomplishments
feel invisible if they aren't
right in front,

sometimes you burn out from
an unbalanced scale of effort
and pay-off.

sometimes
you're not pleased with you,
too tough on you,

never feeling *good enough.*

acknowledge your brilliance
on the smallest of scales,
be patient with you and
let new dreams set sail.

kim rashidi

fortunate

STRENGTH

with the power of eternity
above you,
and the solidity of earth
below you,

you walk the path of
self-assurance with grace.

the toughest tasks seem
like light-work to you.

how did you get this way?

trust,

in yourself.
in your
deeper,
inner
knowing.

think like this, become like this.

kim rashidi

21

THE HERMIT

learning comes naturally
to those with an inherent
sense of curiosity:

do you feel yourself
wondering what it
means to be alive?

are you pulling into
yourself knowing your
answers are inside?

are you climbing the solo journey,
hoping,
wishing,
surviving
on the fact that you know
what's on the other side?
what's on the other side?

you will only ever know
if you try to find out.

kim rashidi

TEN OF PENTACLES

the way you traveled
is proving successful,
you took the right turns,
and the left ones too.

abundance makes itself cozy
in the crevices of your life,
there is enough for comfort
and there is enough to be rosy about.

alive-ness shines on
you and your loved ones,

more finds its way to you
because you are *you*,
and not what you do.

kim rashidi

fortunate

THE HANGED MAN

wait,

there's something you're not seeing.
a perspective you're missing.
a change you're not anticipating.

heed,

why are you in a stand-still?
reflect on what's not working
in your favour anymore.

shift,

let go of what was and
how it came to be—
something new shines beautifully.

kim rashidi

fortunate

FOUR OF PENTACLES

slouched down,
feeling like what
you have
isn't enough,
scared what you
do have
is running out,

you're consumed
by a physical commodity,
spending your days counting
an arbitrary quantity.

you seem to be planning a little,
budgeting your days and
adjusting your ways,

but, just don't forget to set it aside,
and come back to earth

because *things* don't make up a life.

kim rashidi

fortunate

WHEEL OF FORTUNE

they say
what comes around goes around.

and you'd think it were that simple,
right?

just as easy as one thing
comes, another one goes.

but with all this colour,
angels, and demons,

you must learn:

the wheel is constantly turning,
(at times in your favour).

you have nothing to lose
if you know that it'll all pass.

such is the temporariness of life.

fortunate

THE SUN

a big presence, an overwhelming one.

see how it gives life
to the flowers and lives below?

this life is yours
and with it follows
the yellow of the sky and
the positivity above.

fall into you,
with the certainty that
you too will offer warmth
when you live out your days
with burning passion.

fortunate

NINE OF CUPS

you remain grounded
while accomplishments
parade around
in your mind.

ready for appreciation,
wishes received float
in a few cups.

give thanks for
all that you achieved so far,
give thanks for
all that you attracted so far.

fortunate

TWO OF CUPS

a partnership ensues:

the flow of love is from you, through and
through,

reach for common ground and watch
how abundance comes in twos.

words and the will to stay loyal are what
keep this union in view,

align your insights, and give this fusion its
deserved debut.

SIX OF PENTACLES

the scale of liberty
lets you know that
it will all even out

/when you offer help,
the tables turn
and the same comes
back to you/.

if you're afraid to ask,
gather yourself
and make your case,
knowing that
what connects us all
is our human-ness.

kim rashidi

fortunate

SEVEN OF WANDS

guard yourself
with what you have,
it seems as though
the evil eye may
bat its lash.

nay-sayers attack those
who do as they wish,
nay-sayers stand back and watch
those who flourish,
nay-sayers try to bring you down a notch,

nay-sayers stay saying nay to life.

nay-sayers don't improve,
but you have a plan
and you'll move on up.

nay-sayers can't hold you back.

those who don't wish you well,
aren't well themselves.

kim rashidi

THE HIEROPHANT

you'll know when to use
your secret weapon,

a weapon is a tool is a weapon is a portal.

knowledge acts as the key:
sometimes unlocking
paths not meant for you,
and in turn illuminating
the ones that are.

either direction your destiny calls,
collect information at each pit stop,

you never know what won't be of use
or what might become a dignified muse
when deciding your truths.

fortunate

THE FOOL

you're at the start line,
but sit back
and breathe.

with the ease of ignorance,
you slip into something new,

challenges and rewards
will be there, too.

after all, this is a *journey*
you're taking on,

what sparks your curiosity
fuels your humanity;
let that interest take you away,
and the rest will seem like play.

kim rashidi

fortunate

FIVE OF CUPS

worried with what's in front of
you, you fail to see other
options, and even your dreams
across the horizon.

you may have gotten distracted,
been too much so in your ego,

take a step back,
be present,
and think.
* * *
don't cry over spilled milk
when you never liked it to begin with.

TEN OF SWORDS

as time loops
and life
(and love
and lore)
halt,
find the peace in such subtractions.

a life with less isn't a lesser life.
perhaps it's deceit disguised
as a bullet, dodged.

find a way to be
while being without.

fortunate

unfulfilled by what
you thought should bring joy,

you turn your back
and walk away
to mountains unknown.

leave
resentment behind.
and find
what you love,

this isn't a mystery
for you to solve,

just follow your heart.

kim rashidi

THE EMPEROR

holding life and reality
in your very own hands,
you show others
what it means
to make decisions
with conviction.

you hold the calmness
that comes before the storm,
and unleash it when
you see fit,

your expertise lights the way,
and those in your circle will
never be led astray.

fortunate

with your hair in the wind,
you're already in motion,
already starting your quest
just with your fascination.

bit by bit,
your paradigm shifts,

and you begin

to look at life as an event
in which you can live
out your heart's content.

kim rashidi

fortunate

FOUR OF SWORDS

when you close your eyes
(you should close your eyes),
you enter a space that's just for you.

maybe you need to make room
for rest and relaxation and meditation,

maybe life will make the room for you.

do as asked (by your body, by your soul).

think it through,
whatever *it* may be.

there's always an it.

closing your eyes
(physically, metaphysically)
means that you will open them again,

and you'll see that same *it*
in a way
that doesn't exhaust you anymore.

kim rashidi

39

FIVE OF WANDS

conflicted by those around you,

your distracted *what ifs*
made you forget
that you and yours
are one and the same.

change is nothing to be
afraid of,

love is nothing to shy
away from.

THE STAR

replenishing the soul
and the senses,
your life looks like a glowing
renewal of consciousness.

you finally *feel*
in that mesmerizing way
where everything is beautiful,
lively, and *possible*.
* * *
seize this life,
day by day, star by star,
and soon enough
you'll find yourself
at your highest bar.

ACE OF PENTACLES

seemingly out of nowhere,
an opportunity
presents itself.

and right through its golden
arches,
livelihood awaits.

step through with gratitude,
and find your footing
without having assumed
that this is forever-hood.

PAGE OF WANDS

tweaking an idea
is your way of
breaking it out
into the world.

a part of your
creativity is from earth,
grounded and humbled,
the other is from out and above,
grandiose and doubled,

contemplate
a balance between the two,
then, follow in your own footsteps;
you'll know what to do.

SEVEN OF SWORDS

sneaking away with what
you believe is yours,

you s t o p.
you look back
at what was,
at what could have been.

maybe it's a strategy
you're conjuring,
maybe it's a betrayal
you're escaping.
* * *
you leave behind an ounce of
who you are or what you own,
but,
either or both will come back to
you different or renewed.

fortunate

THREE OF WANDS

by fantasizing possibilities,
you
paint your future
with the brush of luck.

you create an existence
by learning through life.

by expanding your horizons,
the entire universe

(mind
body
soul)

is with you on this one.

kim rashidi

fortunate

the ship has sailed.

but, plot twist!
you're on it.

it's not too late, it never was:
go into the unknown,
and release the beliefs
that show you no mercy.

reach for support
and you won't ever come short.

fortunate

KING OF SWORDS

clear sky,
clear mind.

you carry a light,
but, oh, so heavily.

focus on yourself tonight.

clear sky,
clear mind,

lead with what you know
and ask when you don't.

pique their interest tomorrow.

kim rashidi

JUSTICE

balancing *thinking* and *doing*,
you sample the life
of doing what's *right*.

faced with tough decisions,
you weigh out
how it should be
and
how it simply is.

you need not ration
your love nor your support,

show yourself the same
compassion that you do
to others.

fortunate

THE EMPRESS

abundance is only abundant
when it is welcome,

call on your receptive nature
and invite her in:
nurture and create
what you see as a win.

this act of self-love is
your duty to reality,

a simple thank you will do,
along with the belief
that you *deserve* it, too.

fortunate

SEVEN OF CUPS

paths glisten ahead of you
beaming with opportunity,

they may all *seem* great
but tread with caution,
 some things are not what
they appear to be.

peel a layer back,
and analyze,
you'll see that
some rots are hidden
behind jewelry.

don't be scared,
just be aware.

kim rashidi

fortunate

ACE OF WANDS

inspiration doesn't come easy,
but for you it slips into
the moment with such ease
that it makes you think it belongs here.

follow your own lead,
craft your ideas and
manifest them into reality.

with no time you'll
see how the ideas you
planted blossom into a
beautiful tree.

you weave an intricate masterpiece,

and so goes the story of your life.

kim rashidi

fortunate

EIGHT OF PENTACLES

thank yourself
for working on you,

for cultivating your skills
and your knowledge, too.

mastery over yourself
strings along
the want to
improve and learn—

the skill with the most return.

fortunate

if it feels like you're carrying
the weight of the world,
you most likely are.

something needs to change,
and time needs to be made

for you to slip into life
rather than carry on
with pains you
need not claim.

an end is near
and your labour will pay off,

think of when you'll look back,
how will you say that you
spent your time:

was happiness an act,
or were you truly sublime?

kim rashidi

fortunate

THE CHARIOT

with your morals in check
and your thought process aligned,

making decisions and going places
intuitively interlaces.

you have a balance of
all that you need,

commit to staying on track and
doing what makes you feel bright,

surely, the result will be a delight.

fortunate

THE HIGH PRIESTESS

everything you could ever want
has been summoned to your feet,
the moon, the world, all its energy,

all you have to *do* is
be open to receive.

ideas of inadequacy
may float around,
pay them no attention
and *poof* away, they shall.

your subconscious begs you
for a visit into its depths,

pay your respects
by treating yourself
to an inward journey,
from which you'll come
out of feeling worthy.

kim rashidi

THE MOON

don't be fooled by shadows
that roam (in the night).

the moon hides its white
and leaves half the world
relying on man-made light.

these illusions may seem
real. but be weary,
they are merely one
side of a story.

trust the light within:
your intuition,
you may call it,

with guidance
you'll cast away all
unsavoury silhouettes.

kim rashidi

fortunate

QUEEN OF CUPS

you might as well be
a part of the ocean
with how effortlessly
you flow in between states
of human and Being.

your creativity paints
each sunrise true and gives
meaning to the death of day,

and because you care so deeply,
nothing can ever go astray.

it might be overwhelming
to emote this much,

so, find a way to make
your feelings make sense;
then, so will everything else.

kim rashidi

fortunate

what you feel about yourself
and what you feel about others
are in harmonious same-ness.

with love to go around
and love to come back,
choices look like
blissful rejoices.

guided by love,
the highest energy of all,
the earth and the mountains
will chime in
and move to the right place
just for you to meet
life honestly
and let it reveal its true face.

kim rashidi

58

fortunate

NINE OF WANDS

you're faced with
a final test,

but don't give up just yet!

push aside the *no*s
and the worry,

every second you've spent
has been worth the journey.

with one more step and one
more swing at chance,

finish what you started
and revel in its romance.

kim rashidi

fortunate

you're done!
you went through it
and came out alive.

accomplishments float around
you and give off a high.

reflect
on all that you learned
and on all that you gained,

write it down or paint it out,
bring concepts to life, and
banish the core of your doubt.

kim rashidi

FOUR OF WANDS

maybe you lost your mind
momentarily,
maybe you let go of it
temporarily,

maybe you found home
in someone else,
maybe you created
joy with less.

regardless of past events,
this is a homecoming
and you're coming to

your senses,
your mind,
your life.

make security a priority and
stability shall arrive with surety.

fortunate

a period of time in which you are
at ease is due,

abundance paints your life with plush
fates like a hue,

the yellow of the sun and the yellow
of gold both invite you in to enjoy.

    be bold and claim what's yours;
    fall no victim to flashy detours.

fortunate

QUEEN OF PENTACLES

admiring what you've created,
you smile because
you have the power
to conjure the same
time and time again.

you've harnessed the
energy of a can-do adult:
perfecting all aspects of
domestic life.

offer your kindness
to those who ask and
those who don't
(and especially yourself).

you moved continents
and can show others how,
but just relax for now.

kim rashidi

fortunate

EIGHT OF SWORDS

your prison or hell is created by you
and you alone.

holding you back are negative lies,
limiting beliefs, and
formless thoughts.

you feed into them and they feed into
you.

* * *

it's time
to flee the mental cage that
you bound yourself in

and ease the blindfold that
makes the world seem so dim.

find beauty in
the small moments of
life,

get out of your head,
and fall into love.

kim rashidi

fortunate

lost in the reality
of living in reality,
you stop yourself from seeing
it as it is.

living in a diluted vision,
you struggle to make the
choices that need to be made.

don't let options stress you,
break free from the
worldview that a decision
can be so fatal.

each choice made is an
experience gained,
and there's nothing wrong
with racking up stories to share
and even having a few to spare.

kim rashidi

65

fortunate

THE MAGICIAN

ponder into your tool belt and
pull out a few things:
trust in yourself,
and a love that
knows no limits.

your ideas and thoughts
permeate reality, they
sprinkle themselves into
mortality, they
manifest their sequences
through spirituality;

this is your power
as a human being:
you bring in your *actuality*.

keep your intentions in line,
and you'll be just fine.

FIVE OF SWORDS

you might be consumed
with collecting
more eggs in your basket,
more swords on your side,
more satisfaction in life.

wanting to be right
more than
wanting to learn
is an issue of concern;

check with yourself:

is every battle worth the fight,
could you go on
without being right?

kim rashidi

fortunate

victory is just in your grasp,
and with it comes
confidence.

but there's a consequence:

being in the public eye
has both its pros and cons,
and with every action,
a reaction corresponds.

remain grounded
and keep ahead,
you've done great so far,
but you're not quite done yet.

kim rashidi

fortunate

THE TOWER

things can get blurry,
when
life falls apart and
events go wrong,

but don't worry,

your next start
won't be too long.
* * *
shedding layers to make room,
take this time to rest
and reset. find a new angle
and become your best.

fortunate

TWO OF WANDS

if you want the world in your hands
and your future to expand,
paint your reality through decisions
powered by inspired visions.

take the necessary actions,
in due time.
discover your own way of life,
in due time.

wherever you may be,
you're there *early*,
you've got the time
to plan it out
and see it through.

it's all up to you.

kim rashidi

QUEEN OF WANDS

cloaked in luxury,
step into your power,

exude your gifted charm,
and be as bold as a ruler.

you worked hard
to get where you are,
now feast on all that *here*
brings on.

limiting beliefs
have got you torn,
find what
withholds royalty
and make it adjourn.

kim rashidi

fortunate

KNIGHT OF SWORDS

your thoughts, ideas,
and actions
move at a speed that
you warmed up for.

nothing
stands in your way
as long as you have
you to depend on.
* * *
your course of action
is a little unclear,
do do do
isn't productive
if you have no clue
of the intent behind
what you're trying to pursue.

take the time to think it out,
you'll make all the clearer your route.

kim rashidi

fortunate

KING OF PENTACLES

disciplined and ready,
tell yourself
i can do this
and mean it, too.

your acts of creation
are at their completion,
and it just goes to show
that the material world

is no longer on hold—
everything here is for you to relish,
the present
moment is for you to cherish.

kim rashidi

fortunate

in a mysterious turn of events,
where not every detail is yet revealed,

draw on the power of help.
don't settle into solo-mentality.

yes, you can do things alone,
but what's the use when others can
help and lighten the load?

kim rashidi

fortunate

TEN OF CUPS

admire the alignment you're in
whether at home,
love, work, or school.

challenges were faced
(or are to be conquered),
with ultimate symmetry,

so, raise your glass
in cheers of who you are,

and follow yourself into
opportunities that
light up your life.

kim rashidi

fortunate

with a mind clouded by
sharp objects,
it might be heavy
to think straight,
to think happy.

but to identify with the
thoughts is another thing
than to have the thoughts
in the first place.

do not claim what does not serve you,

let intrusive thoughts
be in passing,
and let them
act as a reminder to
identify with what
does serve you,

life as you.

kim rashidi

JUDGEMENT

you—stuck on this earth.

your higher self—at ease, knowing
what's for you will come to you,

they invite earth-you
to rise above
the judgements of earth-bound life
and see existence with
a fresh pair of eyes.

give advice
to yourself from a
place of no labels
—no good, no bad—

and perhaps
at the end of the day,
you'll be of aid to
someone else
through the cosmic knowledge
of trusting yourself.

kim rashidi

fortunate

FOUR OF CUPS

distracted by what's
immediately possible,
you may not see all
that life has to offer.

maybe you didn't know
such things existed,
maybe you weren't
ready to part ways
with old habits.

but now is the time
to see what checks your
boxes
and what leaves them
blank,

and go on
with a list that
tells your tale
in a way that
creates your fate.

kim rashidi

fortunate

kim rashidi

fortunate

kim rashidi

fortunate

kim rashidi

Made in the USA
Monee, IL
08 March 2021